U.S. Department of Justice
Office of Justice Programs
810 Seventh Street N.W.
Washington, DC 20531

Michael B. Mukasey
Attorney General

Jeffrey L. Sedgwick
Acting Assistant Attorney General

David W. Hagy
Director, National Institute of Justice

This and other publications and products of the
National Institute of Justice can be found at:

National Institute of Justice
www.ojp.usdoj.gov/nij

Office of Justice Programs
Innovation • Partnerships • Safer Neighborhoods
www.ojp.usdoj.gov

APR. 08

Electronic Crime Scene Investigation:
A Guide for First Responders,
Second Edition

NCJ 219941

David W. Hagy
Director, National Institute of Justice

Contents

Introduction

This guide is intended to assist State and local law enforcement and other first responders who may be responsible for preserving an electronic crime scene and for recognizing, collecting, and safeguarding digital evidence. It is not all inclusive but addresses situations encountered with electronic crime scenes and digital evidence. All crime scenes are unique and the judgment of the first responder, agency protocols, and prevailing technology should all be considered when implementing the information in this guide. First responders to electronic crime scenes should adjust their practices as circumstances—including level of experience, conditions, and available equipment—warrant. The circumstances of individual crime scenes and Federal, State, and local laws may dictate actions or a particular order of actions other than those described in this guide. First responders should be familiar with all the information in this guide and perform their duties and responsibilities as circumstances dictate.

When dealing with digital evidence, general forensic and procedural principles should be applied:

- The process of collecting, securing, and transporting digital evidence should not change the evidence.

- Digital evidence should be examined only by those trained specifically for that purpose.

- Everything done during the seizure, transportation, and storage of digital evidence should be fully documented, preserved, and available for review.

First responders must use caution when they seize electronic devices. Improperly accessing data stored on electronic devices may violate Federal laws, including the Electronic Communications Privacy Act of 1986 and the Privacy Protection Act of 1980. First responders may need to obtain additional legal authority before they proceed. They should consult the prosecuting attorney for the appropriate jurisdiction to ensure that they have proper legal authority to seize the digital evidence at the scene.

In addition to the legal ramifications of improperly accessing data that is stored on a computer, first responders must understand that computer data and other digital evidence are fragile. Only properly trained personnel should attempt to examine and analyze digital evidence.

> **NOTE:** Officer safety and the safety of others should remain the primary consideration of first responders. Nothing in this guide is intended to be, or should be construed as being, a higher priority than officer safety or the safety of others.

Using This Guide

 When the STOP sign is encountered in this guide, the first responder is advised to STOP, review the corresponding information, and proceed accordingly.

 When the YIELD sign is encountered in this guide, the first responder is advised to review the corresponding information and proceed accordingly.

Intended Audience for This Guide

- Anyone who may encounter a crime scene that might involve digital evidence.

- Everyone who processes a crime scene that includes digital evidence.

- Everyone who supervises personnel who process such crime scenes.

- Everyone who manages an organization that processes such crime scenes.

What Is Digital Evidence?

Digital evidence is information and data of value to an investigation that is stored on, received, or transmitted by an electronic device. This evidence is acquired when data or electronic devices are seized and secured for examination.

Digital evidence—

■ Is latent, like fingerprints or DNA evidence.

■ Crosses jurisdictional borders quickly and easily.

■ Is easily altered, damaged, or destroyed.

■ Can be time sensitive.

NOTE: First responders should remember that digital evidence may also contain physical evidence such as DNA, fingerprints, or serology. Physical evidence should be preserved for appropriate examination.

Handling Digital Evidence at the Scene

Precautions should be taken in the collection, preservation, and transportation of digital evidence. First responders may follow the steps listed below to guide their handling of digital evidence at an electronic crime scene:

■ Recognize, identify, seize, and secure all digital evidence at the scene.

■ Document the entire scene and the specific location of the evidence found.

■ Collect, label, and preserve the digital evidence.

■ Package and transport digital evidence in a secure manner.

Before collecting evidence at a crime scene, first responders should ensure that—

- Legal authority exists to seize evidence.

- The scene has been secured and documented.

- Appropriate personal protective equipment is used.

First responders without the proper training and skills should not attempt to explore the contents of or to recover information from a computer or other electronic device other than to record what is visible on the display screen. Do not press any keys or click the mouse.

Is Your Agency Prepared to Handle Digital Evidence?

Every agency should identify personnel—before they are needed—who have advanced skills, training, experience, and qualifications in handling electronic devices and digital evidence. These experts should be available for situations that exceed the technical expertise of the first responder or agency. This preparation and use is similar to the provisions in place for biohazard and critical incident responses. It is recommended that protocols for how to handle electronic crime scenes and digital evidence be developed in compliance with agency policies and prevailing Federal, State, and local laws and regulations. In particular, under the Privacy Protection Act of 1980, with certain exceptions, law enforcement is prohibited from seizing material from a person who has a legal right to disseminate it to the public. For example, seizure of first amendment material such as drafts of newsletters or Web pages may violate the Privacy Protection Act of 1980.

This guide was developed to assist law enforcement and other first responders when they encounter electronic crime scenes. These guidelines will help first responders—

■ Ensure that officer safety and the safety of others remain the highest priority.

■ Recognize the investigative value of digital evidence.

■ Assess available resources.

■ Identify the equipment and supplies that should be taken to electronic crime scenes.

■ Assess the crime scene and the digital evidence present.

■ Designate the assignments, roles, and responsibilities of personnel involved in the investigation.

Chapter 1. Electronic Devices: Types, Description, and Potential Evidence

Internally attached computer hard drives, external drives, and other electronic devices at a crime scene may contain information that can be useful as evidence in a criminal investigation or prosecution. The devices themselves and the information they contain may be used as digital evidence. In this chapter, such devices will be identified, along with general information about their evidential value.

Some devices require internal or external power to maintain stored information. For these devices, the power must be maintained to preserve the information stored. For additional information about maintaining power to these devices, please refer to chapter 3 of this guide, the device manufacturer's Web site, or other reliable sources of information.

Computer Systems

Description: A computer system consists of hardware and software that process data and is likely to include:

- A case that contains circuit boards, microprocessors, hard drive, memory, and interface connections.

- A monitor or video display device.

- A keyboard.

- A mouse.

- Peripheral or externally connected drives, devices, and components.

Computer systems can take many forms, such as laptops, desktops, tower computers, rack-mounted systems, minicomputers, and mainframe computers. Additional components and peripheral devices include modems, routers, printers, scanners, and docking stations. Many of these are discussed further in this chapter.

Types of Computer Systems

PC, monitor, keyboard, and mouse

Apple G3 computer, monitor, keyboard, and mouse

Apple iMac, keyboard, and mouse

Laptop computer

Potential evidence: A computer system and its components can be valuable evidence in an investigation. The hardware, software, documents, photos, image files, e-mail and attachments, databases, financial information, Internet browsing history, chat logs, buddy lists, event logs, data stored on external devices, and identifying information associated with the computer system and components are all potential evidence.

Storage Devices

Description: Storage devices vary in size and the manner in which they store and retain data. First responders must understand that, regardless of their size or type, these devices may contain information that is valuable to an investigation or prosecution. The following storage devices may be digital evidence:

- **Hard drives.** Hard drives are data storage devices that consist of an external circuit board; external data and power connections; and internal magnetically charged glass, ceramic, or metal platters that store data. First responders may also find hard drives at the scene that are not connected to or installed on a computer. These loose hard drives may still contain valuable evidence.

Types of Hard Drives

SCSI drives   SATA drive   IDE drive   Laptop hard drives

IDE 40-pin   2.5" IDE 44-pin

IDE power and data connections

Serial ATA (SATA)

SCSI HD 68-pin   SCSI IDC 50-pin

3

■ **External hard drives.** Hard drives can also be installed in
an external drive case. External hard drives increase the
computer's data storage capacity and provide the user with
portable data. Generally, external hard drives require a
power supply and a universal serial bus (USB), FireWire,
Ethernet, or wireless connection to a computer system.

External Hard Drive Cases

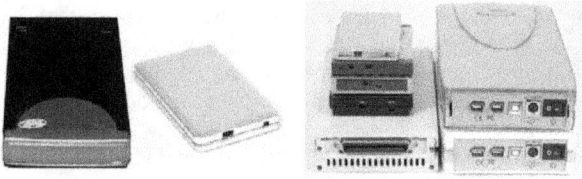

3.5" Hard drive   2.5" Hard drive

Network storage device

■ **Removable media.** Removable media are cartridges and
disk-based data storage devices. They are typically used to
store, archive, transfer, and transport data and other information. These devices help users share data, information,
applications, and utilities among different computers and
other devices.

Removable Media

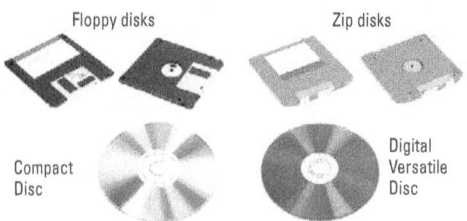

Floppy disks   Zip disks

Compact   Digital
Disc   Versatile
                 Disc

■ **Thumb drives.** Thumb drives are small, lightweight, removable data storage devices with USB connections. These devices, also referred to as flash drives, are easy to conceal and transport. They can be found as part of, or disguised as, a wristwatch, a pocket-size multitool such as a Swiss Army knife, a keychain fob, or any number of common and unique devices.

Common Thumb Drives

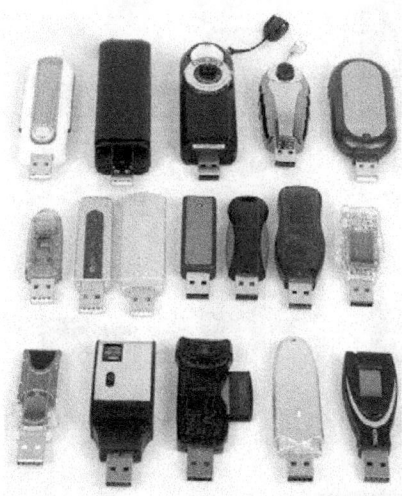

Other Types of Thumb Drives

■ **Memory cards.** Memory cards are small data storage devices commonly used with digital cameras, computers, mobile phones, digital music players, personal digital assistants (PDAs), video game consoles, and handheld and other electronic devices.

Memory Cards

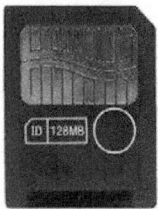

Smart media (SM) card

Secure digital (SD) card

Mini secure digital card

Micro secure digital card

Memory stick

Compact flash card

Potential evidence: Storage devices such as hard drives, external hard drives, removable media, thumb drives, and memory cards may contain information such as e-mail messages, Internet browsing history, Internet chat logs and buddy lists, photographs, image files, databases, financial records, and event logs that can be valuable evidence in an investigation or prosecution.

Handheld Devices

Description: Handheld devices are portable data storage devices that provide communications, digital photography, navigation systems, entertainment, data storage, and personal information management.

Handheld Devices

7

Potential evidence: Handheld devices such as mobile phones, smart phones, PDAs, digital multimedia (audio and video) devices, pagers, digital cameras, and global positioning system (GPS) receivers may contain software applications, data, and information such as documents, e-mail messages, Internet browsing history, Internet chat logs and buddy lists, photographs, image files, databases, and financial records that are valuable evidence in an investigation or prosecution.

 It is important to note that—

- Data or digital evidence may be lost if power is not maintained.

- Data or digital evidence on some devices such as mobile or smart phones can be overwritten or deleted while the device remains activated.

- Software is available for mobile and smart phones that can be activated remotely to render the device unusable and make the data it contains inaccessible if the phone is lost or stolen. This software can produce similar results if activated on a device seized by law enforcement. First responders should take precautions to prevent the loss of data on devices they seize as evidence.

Peripheral Devices

Description: Peripheral devices are equipment that can be connected to a computer or computer system to enhance user access and expand the computer's functions.

Peripheral Devices

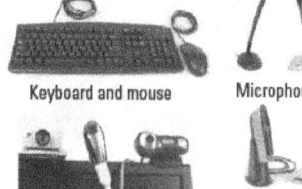
Keyboard and mouse

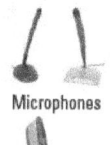
Microphones

USB and FireWire hubs

Web cameras

Memory card readers

VoIP devices

Potential evidence: The devices themselves and the functions they perform or facilitate are all potential evidence. Information stored on the device regarding its use also is evidence, such as incoming and outgoing phone and fax numbers; recently scanned, faxed, or printed documents; and information about the purpose for or use of the device. In addition, these devices can be sources of fingerprints, DNA, and other identifiers.

Other Potential Sources of Digital Evidence

Description: First responders should be aware of and consider as potential evidence other elements of the crime scene that are related to digital information, such as electronic devices, equipment, software, hardware, or other technology that can function independently, in conjunction with, or attached to computer systems. These items may be used to enhance the user's access of and expand the functionality of the computer system, the device itself, or other equipment.

Data storage tape drives   Surveillance equipment

Digital cameras   Video cameras

Digital audio recorders   Digital video recorders

MP3 players

Satellite audio, video receiver, and access cards

Video game consoles

Computer chat headset

Keyboard, mouse, and video (KM) sharing switch

Sim card reader

Global Positioning System (GPS) receiver

Thumb print reader

Reference material

Potential evidence: The device or item itself, its intended or actual use, its functions or capabilities, and any settings or other information it may contain is potential evidence.

Computer Networks

Description: A computer network consists of two or more computers linked by data cables or by wireless connections that share or are capable of sharing resources and data. A computer network often includes printers, other peripheral devices, and data routing devices such as hubs, switches, and routers.

Computer Networks

Network hub

Laptop network card and ethernet cable

Network switch and power supply

Internet modems

Wireless access points

Wireless network server

Wireless cards and devices

Wireless card for PC

Wireless USB device

Directional antenna for wireless card

11

Potential evidence: The networked computers and connected devices themselves may be evidence that is useful to an investigation or prosecution. The data they contain may also be valuable evidence and may include software, documents, photos, image files, e-mail messages and attachments, databases, financial information, Internet browsing history, log files, event and chat logs, buddy lists, and data stored on external devices. The device functions, capabilities, and any identifying information associated with the computer system; components and connections, including Internet protocol (IP) and local area network (LAN) addresses associated with the computers and devices; broadcast settings; and media access card (MAC) or network interface card (NIC) addresses may all be useful as evidence.

Chapter 2. Investigative Tools and Equipment

In most cases, items or devices containing digital evidence can be collected using standard seizure tools and materials. First responders must use caution when collecting, packaging, or storing digital devices to avoid altering, damaging, or destroying the digital evidence. Avoid using any tools or materials that may produce or emit static electricity or a magnetic field as these may damage or destroy the evidence.

Should the complexity of an electronic crime scene exceed the expertise of a first responder, the first responder should request assistance from personnel with advanced equipment and training in digital evidence collection. The technical resource list at www.ecpi-us.org/Technicalresources.html provides additional information for these situations.

Tools and Materials for Collecting Digital Evidence

In addition to tools for processing crime scenes in general, first responders should have the following items in their digital evidence collection toolkit:

- Cameras (photo and video).

- Cardboard boxes.

- Notepads.

- Gloves.

- Evidence inventory logs.

- Evidence tape.

- Paper evidence bags.

- Evidence stickers, labels, or tags.

- Crime scene tape.

- Antistatic bags.

- Permanent markers.

- Nonmagnetic tools.

First responders should also have radio frequency-shielding material such as faraday isolation bags or aluminum foil to wrap cell phones, smart phones, and other mobile communication devices after they have been seized. Wrapping the phones in radio frequency-shielding material prevents the phones from receiving a call, text message, or other communications signal that may alter the evidence.

Collection Tools

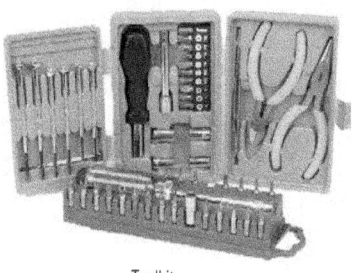

Toolkit   Antistatic Bag

Chapter 3. Securing and Evaluating the Scene

The first responder's primary consideration should be officer safety and the safety of everyone at the crime scene. All actions and activities carried out at the scene should be in compliance with departmental policy as well as Federal, State, and local laws.

After securing the scene and all persons at the scene, the first responder should visually identify all potential evidence and ensure that the integrity of both the digital and traditional evidence is preserved. Digital evidence on computers and other electronic devices can be easily altered, deleted, or destroyed. First responders should document, photograph, and secure digital evidence as soon as possible at the scene.

When securing and evaluating the scene, the first responder should—

■ Follow departmental policy for securing crime scenes.

■ Immediately secure *all* electronic devices, including personal or portable devices.

■ Ensure that no unauthorized person has access to any electronic devices at the crime scene.

■ Refuse offers of help or technical assistance from any unauthorized persons.

■ Remove all persons from the crime scene or the immediate area from which evidence is to be collected.

■ Ensure that the condition of any electronic device is not altered.

■ Leave a computer or electronic device off if it is already turned off.

Components such as keyboard, mouse, removable storage media, and other items may hold latent evidence such as fingerprints, DNA, or other physical evidence that should be preserved. First responders should take the appropriate steps to ensure that physical evidence is not compromised during documentation.

If a computer is on or the power state cannot be determined, the first responder should—

■ Look and listen for indications that the computer is powered on. Listen for the sound of fans running, drives spinning, or check to see if light emitting diodes (LEDs) are on.

■ Check the display screen for signs that digital evidence is being destroyed. Words to look out for include "delete," "format," "remove," "copy," "move," "cut," or "wipe."

■ Look for indications that the computer is being accessed from a remote computer or device.

■ Look for signs of active or ongoing communications with other computers or users such as instant messaging windows or chat rooms.

■ Take note of all cameras or Web cameras (Web cams) and determine if they are active.

Developments in technology and the convergence of communications capabilities have linked even the most conventional devices and services to each other, to computers, and to the Internet. This rapidly changing environment makes it essential for the first responder to be aware of the potential digital evidence in telephones, digital video recorders, other household appliances, and motor vehicles.

Preliminary Interviews

First responders should separate and identify all adult persons of interest at the crime scene and record their location at the time of entry onto the scene.

 No one should be allowed access to any computer or electronic device.

Within the parameters of the agency's policies and applicable Federal, State, and local laws, first responders should obtain as much information from these individuals as possible, including:

- Names of all users of the computers and devices.

- All computer and Internet user information.

- All login names and user account names.

- Purpose and uses of computers and devices.

- All passwords.

- Any automated applications in use.

- Type of Internet access.

- Any offsite storage.

- Internet service provider.

- Installed software documentation.

- All e-mail accounts.

- Security provisions in use.

- Web mail account information.

- Data access restrictions in place.

- All instant message screen names.

- All destructive devices or software in use.

- MySpace, Facebook, or other online social networking Web site account information.

- Any other relevant information.

Chapter 4. Documenting the Scene

 This chapter provides recommendations on documenting or creating a record of an electronic crime scene. The information provided in this guide is not intended to supersede or supplant applicable laws or agency policies.

Documentation of a crime scene creates a record for the investigation. It is important to accurately record the location of the scene; the scene itself; the state, power status, and condition of computers, storage media, wireless network devices, mobile phones, smart phones, PDAs, and other data storage devices; Internet and network access; and other electronic devices. The first responder should be aware that not all digital evidence may be in close proximity to the computer or other devices.

Officials may need to move a computer or another electronic device to find its serial numbers or other identifiers. Moving a computer or another electronic device while it is on may damage it or the digital evidence it contains. Computers and other electronic devices should not be moved until they are powered off. Additional documentation of the system and devices may be performed during the collection phase discussed in chapter 5.

The initial documentation of the scene should include a detailed record using video, photography, and notes and sketches to help recreate or convey the details of the scene later. All activity and processes on display screens should be fully documented.

Documentation of the scene should include the entire location, including the type, location, and position of computers, their components and peripheral equipment, and other electronic devices. The scene may expand to multiple locations; first responders should document all physical connections to and from the computers and other devices.

Record any network and wireless access points that may be present and capable of linking computers and other devices to each other and the Internet. The existence of network and wireless access points may indicate that additional evidence exists beyond the initial scene.

Some circumstances may not permit first responders to collect all electronic devices or components at a scene or location. Applicable laws, agency policies, or other factors may prohibit collecting some computer systems and other electronic devices and the information they contain; however, these devices should be included in the first responder's documentation of the scene.

Chapter 5. Evidence Collection

The first responder must have proper authority—such as plain view observation, consent, or a court order—to search for and collect evidence at an electronic crime scene. The first responder must be able to identify the authority under which he or she may seize evidence and should follow agency guidelines, consult a superior, or contact a prosecutor if a question of appropriate authority arises.

Digital evidence must be handled carefully to preserve the integrity of the physical device as well as the data it contains. Some digital evidence requires special collection, packaging, and transportation techniques. Data can be damaged or altered by electromagnetic fields such as those generated by static electricity, magnets, radio transmitters, and other devices. Communication devices such as mobile phones, smart phones, PDAs, and pagers should be secured and prevented from receiving or transmitting data once they are identified and collected as evidence.

 NOTE: If data encryption is in use on a computer, data storage device, or other electronic device and it is improperly powered off during digital evidence collection, the data it contains may become inaccessible.

Computers, Components, and Devices

To prevent the alteration of digital evidence during collection, first responders should first—

- Document any activity on the computer, components, or devices.

21

- Confirm the power state of the computer. Check for flashing lights, running fans, and other sounds that indicate the computer or electronic device is powered on. If the power state cannot be determined from these indicators, observe the monitor to determine if it is on, off, or in sleep mode.

Assess the Situation

After identifying the computer's power status, follow the steps listed below for the situation most like your own:

Situation 1: The monitor is on. It displays a program, application, work product, picture, e-mail, or Internet site on the screen.

1. Photograph the screen and record the information displayed.

2. Proceed to "If the Computer Is ON" (see P. 25).

Situation 2: The monitor is on and a screen saver or picture is visible.

1. Move the mouse slightly without depressing any buttons or rotating the wheel. Note any onscreen activity that causes the display to change to a login screen, work product, or other visible display.

2. Photograph the screen and record the information displayed.

3. Proceed to "If the Computer Is ON" (see P. 25).

Situation 3: The monitor is on, however, the display is blank as if the monitor is off.

1. Move the mouse slightly without depressing any buttons or rotating the wheel. The display will change from a blank screen to a login screen, work product, or other visible display. Note the change in the display.

2. Photograph the screen and record the information displayed.

3. Proceed to "If the Computer Is ON" (see P. 25).

Situation 4a: The monitor is powered off. The display is blank.

1. If the monitor's power switch is in the off position, turn the monitor on. The display changes from a blank screen to a login screen, work product, or other visible display. Note the change in the display.

2. Photograph the screen and the information displayed.

3. Proceed to "If the Computer Is ON" (see P. 25).

Situation 4b: The monitor is powered off. The display is blank.

4. If the monitor's power switch is in the off position, turn the monitor on. The display does not change; it remains blank. Note that no change in the display occurs.

5. Photograph the blank screen.

6. Proceed to "If the Computer Is OFF" (see P. 24).

Situation 5: The monitor is on. The display is blank.

1. Move the mouse slightly without depressing any buttons or rotating the wheel; wait for a response.

2. If the display does not change and the screen remains blank, confirm that power is being supplied to the monitor. If the display remains blank, check the computer case for active lights, listen for fans spinning or other indications that the computer is on.

3. If the screen remains blank and the computer case gives no indication that the system is powered on, proceed to "If the Computer Is OFF" (see P. 24).

If the Computer Is OFF

For desktop, tower, and minicomputers follow these steps:

1. Document, photograph, and sketch all wires, cables, and other devices connected to the computer.

2. Uniquely label the power supply cord and all cables, wires, or USB drives attached to the computer as well as the corresponding connection each cord, cable, wire, or USB drive occupies on the computer.

3. Photograph the uniquely labeled cords, cables, wires, and USB drives and the corresponding labeled connections.

4. Remove and secure the power supply cord from the back of the computer and from the wall outlet, power strip, or battery backup device.

5. Disconnect and secure all cables, wires, and USB drives from the computer and document the device or equipment connected at the opposite end.

6. Place tape over the floppy disk slot, if present.

7. Make sure that the CD or DVD drive trays are retracted into place; note whether these drive trays are empty, contain disks, or are unchecked; and tape the drive slot closed to prevent it from opening.

8. Place tape over the power switch.

9. Record the make, model, serial numbers, and any user-applied markings or identifiers.

10. Record or log the computer and all its cords, cables, wires, devices, and components according to agency procedures.

11. Package all evidence collected following agency procedures to prevent damage or alteration during transportation and storage.

For laptop computers follow these steps:

1. Document, photograph, and sketch all wires, cables, and devices connected to the laptop computer.

2. Uniquely label all wires, cables, and devices connected to the laptop computer as well as the connection they occupied.

3. Photograph the uniquely labeled cords, cables, wires, and devices connected to the laptop computer and the corresponding labeled connections they occupied.

4. Remove and secure the power supply and all batteries from the laptop computer.

5. Disconnect and secure all cables, wires, and USB drives from the computer and document the equipment or device connected at the opposite end.

6. Place tape over the floppy disk slot, if present.

7. Make sure that the CD or DVD drive trays are retracted into place; note whether these drive trays are empty, contain disks, or are unchecked; and tape the drive slot closed to prevent it from opening.

8. Place tape over the power switch.

9. Record the make, model, serial numbers, and any user-applied markings or identifiers.

10. Record or log the computer and all its cords, cables, wires, devices, and components according to agency procedures.

11. Package all evidence collected following agency procedures to prevent damage or alteration during transportation and storage.

If the Computer Is ON

 For practical purposes, removing the power supply when you seize a computer is generally the safest option. If evidence of a crime is visible on the computer display, however, you may

25

need to request assistance from personnel who have experience in volatile data capture and preservation.

In the following situations, immediate disconnection of power is recommended:

- Information or activity onscreen indicates that data is being deleted or overwritten.

- There is indication that a destructive process is being performed on the computer's data storage devices.

- The system is powered on in a typical Microsoft® Windows® environment. Pulling the power from the back of the computer will preserve information about the last user to login and at what time the login occurred, most recently used documents, most recently used commands, and other valuable information.

 In the following situations, immediate disconnection of power is NOT recommended:

- Data of apparent evidentiary value is in plain view onscreen. The first responder should seek out personnel who have experience and training in capturing and preserving volatile data before proceeding.

- Indications exist that any of the following are active or in use:

  - Chat rooms.

  - Open text documents.

  - Remote data storage.

  - Instant message windows.

  - Child pornography.

  - Contraband.

  - Financial documents.

  - Data encryption.

  - Obvious illegal activities.

For mainframe computers, servers, or a group of networked computers, the first responder should secure the scene and request assistance from personnel who have training in collecting digital evidence from large or complex computer systems. Technical assistance is available at www.ecpi-us.org/Technicalresources.html.

Other Forms of Evidence

Be alert to the crime scene environment. Look out for pieces of paper with possible passwords, handwritten notes, blank pads of paper with impressions from prior writings, hardware and software manuals, calendars, literature, and text or graphic material printed from the computer that may reveal information relevant to the investigation. These forms of evidence also should be documented and preserved in compliance with departmental policies.

Other Electronic and Peripheral Devices of Potential Evidential Value

Electronic devices such as those listed below may contain information of evidentiary value to an investigation. Except in emergency situations, such devices should not be operated and the information they might contain should not be accessed directly. If a situation warrants accessing these devices and the information they contain immediately, all actions taken should be thoroughly documented. Data may be lost if a device is not properly handled or its data properly accessed.

The following are examples of electronic devices, components, and peripherals that first responders may need to collect as digital evidence:

- Audio recorders.

- GPS accessories.

- Answering machines.

- Computer chips.

- Pagers.

- Cordless landline telephones.

- Copy machines.

- Cellular telephones.

- Hard drive duplicators.

- Facsimile (fax) machines.

- Printers.

- Multifunction machines (printer, scanner, copier, and fax).

- Wireless access points.

- Laptop power supplies and accessories.

- Smart cards.

- Videocassette recorders (VCRs).

- Scanners.

- Telephone caller ID units.

- Personal Computer Memory Card International Association (PCMCIA) cards.

- PDAs.

 Special handling may be required to preserve the integrity and evidentiary value of these electronic devices. First responders should secure the devices and request assistance from personnel who have advanced training in collecting digital evidence. Refer to www.ecpi-us.org/Technicalresources.html for more information on advanced technical assistance.

NOTE: When collecting electronic devices, components, and peripherals such as those listed above, remember to collect the power supplies, cables, and adapters for those devices as well.

Collecting Digital Evidence Flow Chart

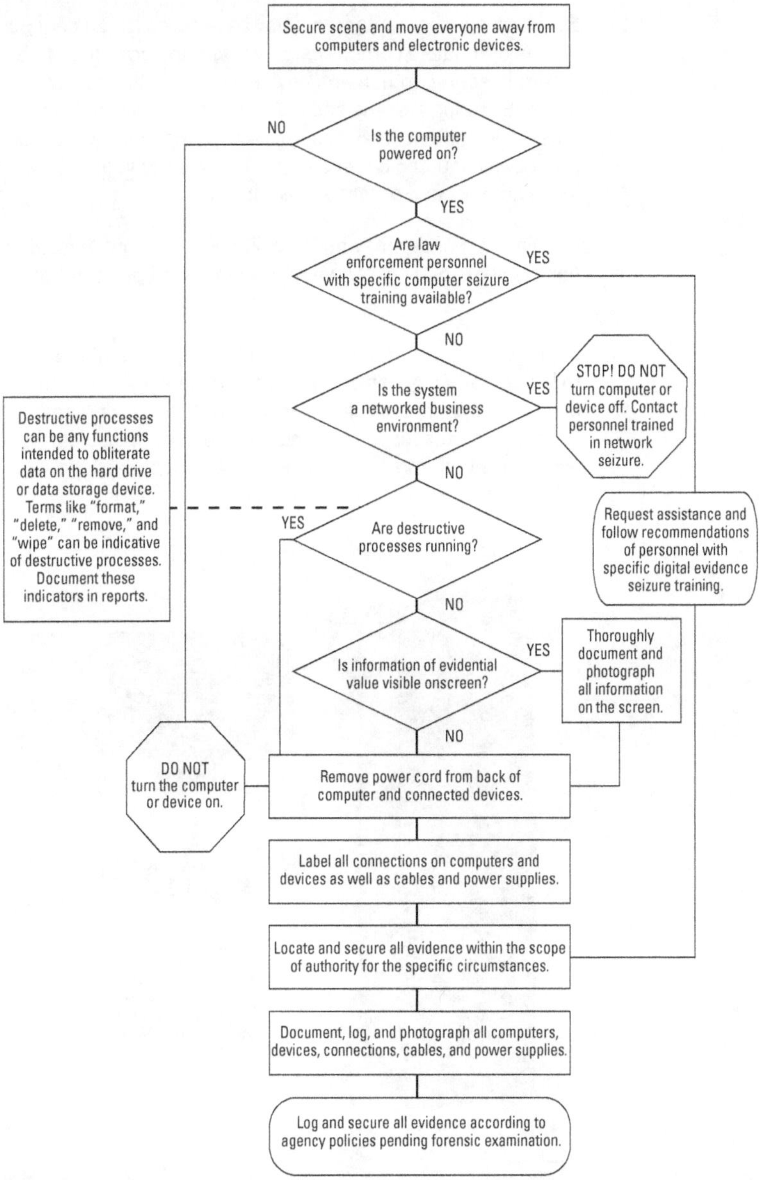

Secure scene and move everyone away from computers and electronic devices.

Is the computer powered on?

NO

YES

Are law enforcement personnel with specific computer seizure training available?

YES

NO

Is the system a networked business environment?

YES

STOP! DO NOT turn computer or device off. Contact personnel trained in network seizure.

NO

Destructive processes can be any functions intended to obliterate data on the hard drive or data storage device. Terms like "format," "delete," "remove," and "wipe" can be indicative of destructive processes. Document these indicators in reports.

YES

Are destructive processes running?

Request assistance and follow recommendations of personnel with specific digital evidence seizure training.

NO

Is information of evidential value visible onscreen?

YES

Thoroughly document and photograph all information on the screen.

NO

DO NOT turn the computer or device on.

Remove power cord from back of computer and connected devices.

Label all connections on computers and devices as well as cables and power supplies.

Locate and secure all evidence within the scope of authority for the specific circumstances.

Document, log, and photograph all computers, devices, connections, cables, and power supplies.

Log and secure all evidence according to agency policies pending forensic examination.

Computers in a Business Environment

Business environments frequently have complicated configurations of multiple computers networked to each other, to a common server, to network devices, or a combination of these. Securing a scene and collecting digital evidence in these environments may pose challenges to the first responder. Improperly shutting down a system may result in lost data, lost evidence, and potential civil liability.

The first responder may find a similar environment in residential locations, particularly when a business is operated from the home.

In some instances, the first responder may encounter unfamiliar operating systems or unique hardware and software configurations that require specific shutdown procedures. Such circumstances are beyond the scope of this guide. For assistance with this type of scene, first responders should refer to www.ecpi-us.org/Technicalresources.html.

Servers

Chapter 6. Packaging, Transportation, and Storage of Digital Evidence

 Digital evidence—and the computers and electronic devices on which it is stored—is fragile and sensitive to extreme temperatures, humidity, physical shock, static electricity, and magnetic fields.

The first responder should take precautions when documenting, photographing, packaging, transporting, and storing digital evidence to avoid altering, damaging, or destroying the data.

Packaging Procedures

All actions related to the identification, collection, packaging, transportation, and storage of digital evidence should be thoroughly documented. When packing digital evidence for transportation, the first responder should—

- Ensure that all digital evidence collected is properly documented, labeled, marked, photographed, video recorded or sketched, and inventoried before it is packaged. All connections and connected devices should be labeled for easy reconfiguration of the system later.

- Remember that digital evidence may also contain latent, trace, or biological evidence and take the appropriate steps to preserve it. Digital evidence imaging should be done before latent, trace, or biological evidence processes are conducted on the evidence.

- Pack all digital evidence in antistatic packaging. Only paper bags and envelopes, cardboard boxes, and antistatic containers should be used for packaging digital evidence. Plastic materials should not be used when collecting digital evidence because plastic can produce or convey static electricity and allow humidity and condensation to develop, which may damage or destroy the evidence.

- Ensure that all digital evidence is packaged in a manner that will prevent it from being bent, scratched, or otherwise deformed.

- Label all containers used to package and store digital evidence clearly and properly.

- Leave cellular, mobile, or smart phone(s) in the power state (on or off) in which they were found.

 ■ Package mobile or smart phone(s) in signal-blocking material such as faraday isolation bags, radio frequency-shielding material, or aluminum foil to prevent data messages from being sent or received by the devices. (First responders should be aware that if inappropriately packaged, or removed from shielded packaging, the device may be able to send and receive data messages if in range of a communication signal.)

- Collect all power supplies and adapters for all electronic devices seized.

Transportation Procedures

When transporting digital evidence, the first responder should—

 ■ Keep digital evidence away from magnetic fields such as those produced by radio transmitters, speaker magnets, and magnetic mount emergency lights. Other potential hazards that the first responder should be aware of include seats heaters and any device or material that can produce static electricity.

- Avoid keeping digital evidence in a vehicle for prolonged periods of time. Heat, cold, and humidity can damage or destroy digital evidence.

- Ensure that computers and electronic devices are packaged and secured during transportation to prevent damage from shock and vibration.

- Document the transportation of the digital evidence and maintain the chain of custody on all evidence transported.

Storage Procedures

When storing digital evidence, the first responder should—

- Ensure that the digital evidence is inventoried in accordance with the agency's policies.

- Ensure that the digital evidence is stored in a secure, climate-controlled environment or a location that is not subject to extreme temperature or humidity.

- Ensure that the digital evidence is not exposed to magnetic fields, moisture, dust, vibration, or any other elements that may damage or destroy it.

NOTE: Potentially valuable digital evidence including dates, times, and system configuration settings may be lost due to prolonged storage if the batteries or power source that preserve this information fails. Where applicable, inform the evidence custodian and the forensic examiner that electronic devices are battery powered and require prompt attention to preserve the data stored in them.

If more than one computer is seized as evidence, all computers, cables, and devices connected to them should be properly labeled to facilitate reassembly if necessary. In this example, the computer is designated as computer A. All connections and cables are marked with an "A" and a unique number.

Subsequently seized computers can be labeled in alphabetical order. The corresponding connections and cables can be labeled with the letter designation for the computer and a unique number to ensure proper reassembly.

Example: Computer A

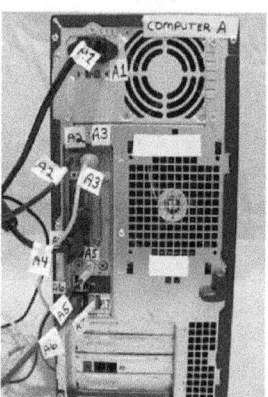

Label computer, all cables, and corresponding connections.

Chapter 7. Electronic Crime and Digital Evidence Considerations by Crime Category

The lists of electronic crime and digital evidence considerations presented in this chapter are not exhaustive, but are intended to assist a first responder identify sources of potentially valuable digital evidence by crime category. Depending on the complexity of the scene and the situation, the first responder may need to request more advanced technical assistance.

In some circumstances, trace, latent, or biological evidence such as fingerprints or DNA that may be important to the investigation may be present on computers and their components or on other electronic devices. First responders should follow agency procedures for collecting such evidence. Any destructive processes associated with recovering or analyzing trace, latent, biological, or other evidence should be postponed until after the digital evidence has been recovered for examination and analysis.

 To assist in the forensic examination, the first responder should document the following information when possible:

■ A summary of the case.

■ Passwords to digital evidence seized.

■ Investigation point-of-contact information.

■ Preliminary reports and documents.

■ Keyword lists.

- Suspected criminal activity.

- Suspect information including nicknames.

Child Abuse or Exploitation

Potential digital evidence in child abuse or child exploitation investigations includes:

- Computers.

- Scanners.

- Mobile communication devices.

- Video and still photo cameras and media.

- Calendars or journals.

- Digital camera software.

- Internet activity records.

- Photo editing and viewing software.

- Printed e-mail, notes, and letters and maps.

- Printed images or pictures.

- Notes or records of chat sessions.

- Web cameras and microphones.

- Computer games.

- Printers and copiers.

- Information regarding steganography.

- Removable media.

- External data storage devices.

- Videotapes.

- Video game consoles, games, and expansion packs.

- References to user-created folders and file names that classify images.

Computer Intrusion

Potential digital evidence in computer intrusion investigations includes:

- Computers.

- Network devices, routers, switches.

- Handheld mobile devices.

- Antennas.

- Removable media.

- External data storage devices.

- Web camera(s).

- Wireless network equipment.

- Lists of contacts and address books.

- Lists of Internet protocol addresses.

- Lists or records of computer intrusion software.

- Records of Internet chat sessions.

- Printed e-mail, notes, and letters.

- Printed computer program code.

- Executable programs.

- Lists of computers accessed.

- Notes or records of Internet activity.

- Usernames and passwords.

Counterfeiting

Potential digital evidence in counterfeiting investigations includes:

- Computers.

- Handheld mobile devices.

- PDAs or address books.

- Information regarding Internet activity.

- Information regarding checks, currency, and money orders.

- Removable media and external data storage devices.

- Credit card magnetic strip reader.

- Online banking software.

- Calendar(s).

- Reproductions of signatures.

- Customer information or credit card data.

- False identification.

- Printed e-mail, notes, and letters.

- False financial transaction forms.

- Information regarding financial records.

- Printouts of databases.

Death Investigation

Potential digital evidence in death investigations includes:

- Computers.

- Internet service bills.

- Removable media.

- External data storage devices.

- Mobile communication devices.

- PDAs.

- Address books and contact information.

- Telephone records.

- Personal writings and diaries.

- Medical records.

- Printed e-mail, notes, and letters.

- Financial or asset records.

- Recently printed material.

- Information regarding legal documents.

- Information regarding Internet activity.

- Will-making software or references.

Domestic Violence, Threats, and Extortion

Potential digital evidence in domestic violence, threats, and extortion investigations includes:

- Computers.

- Removable media.

- User names and accounts.

- External data storage devices.

- Mobile communication devices.

- Telephone records.

- PDAs or address books.

- Financial or asset records.

- Personal writings and diaries.

- Information regarding Internet activity.

- Printed e-mail, notes, and letters.

- Legal documents.

- Caller ID units.

E-mail Threats, Harassment, and Stalking

Potential digital evidence in e-mail threat, harassment, and stalking investigations includes:

- Computers.

- Handheld mobile devices.

- PDAs and address books.

- Telephone records.

- Diaries or records of surveillance.

- Evidence of victim background research.

- E-mail, notes, and letters.

- Financial or asset records.

- Printed photos or images.

- Legal documents.

- Information regarding Internet activity.

- Printed maps.

Gambling

Potential digital evidence in gambling investigations includes:

- Computers.

- Removable media.

- PDA, address books, or contact lists.

- External data storage devices.

- Customer database and bettor records.

- Information regarding Internet activity.

- Electronic money transfers.

- Online banking software.

- Calendars.

- Sports betting statistics.

- Customer information or credit card data.

- Financial asset records.

- Printed e-mail, notes, and letters.

- References to online gambling sites.

Identity Theft

Potential digital evidence in identity theft investigations includes:

- Computers.

- Mobile devices.

- Records of online purchases.

- Removable media.

- External data storage devices.

- PDAs, address books, contact lists.

- Online banking software.

- Information regarding Internet activity.

- Financial asset records.

- Electronic money transfers.

- Laminator(s).

- Calendars or journals.

- Forged documents and false identification.

- Victim information and credit card data.

- Copies of signatures.

- Printed e-mail, notes, and letters.

- ID pictures.

- Check cashing cards.

- Scanner(s).

Narcotics

Potential digital evidence in narcotics investigations includes:

- Computers.

- Handheld mobile devices.

- Removable media.

- External data storage devices.

- PDAs, address books, and contact information.

- Forged identification.

- Databases.

- Information regarding Internet activity.

- Drug receipts.

- Blank prescription forms.

- Printed e-mail, notes, and letters.

- Financial asset records.

- GPS devices.

Online or Economic Fraud

Potential digital evidence in online or economic fraud investigations includes:

- Computers.

- Removable media.

- Mobile communication devices.

- External data storage devices.

- Online auction sites and account data.

- Databases.

- PDAs, address books, and contact lists.

- Printed e-mail, notes, and letters.

- Calendars or journals.

- Financial asset records.

- Accounting or recordkeeping software.

- Printed photos and image files.

- Records or notes of chat sessions.

- Information regarding Internet activity.

- Customer credit information.

- Online banking information.

- List(s) of credit card numbers.

- Telephone numbers and call logs.

- Credit card magnetic strip reader.

- Credit card statements or bills.

- Printers, copiers, and scanners.

Prostitution

Potential digital evidence in prostitution investigations includes:

- Computers.

- Handheld mobile devices.

- Removable media.

- External data storage devices.

- Address books and client lists.

- Customer database or records.

- Calendars or datebooks.

- Forged identification.

- Information regarding Internet activity.

- Financial asset records.

- Printed e-mail, notes, and letters.

- Information regarding Web site.

- Medical records.

- Web camera(s).

Software Piracy

Potential digital evidence in software piracy investigations includes:

- Computers.

- Handheld mobile devices.

- Removable media.

- External data storage devices.

- Information regarding chat sessions.

- Information on cracking software.

- Printed e-mail, notes, and letters.

- References to copyrighted software.

- Forged software certificates.

- Lists of software activation codes.

- Information regarding Internet activity.

- Software duplication and packing material.

Telecommunication Fraud

Potential digital evidence in telecommunication fraud investigations includes:

- Computers.

- Handheld mobile devices.

- Removable media.

- External data storage devices.

- Phone programming software and cables.

- Multiple mobile phones.

- Subscriber identity module (SIM) card reader.

- Hacker boxes and cables.

- Lists of customer database records.

- Stolen telephones.

- Printed e-mail, notes, and letters.

- Financial asset records.

- Information regarding Internet activity.

- Telephone programming manuals.

- Erasable programmable read-only memory (EPROM) burner.

Terrorism (Homeland Security)

Potential digital evidence in terrorism investigations includes:

- Computers.

- Handheld mobile devices.

- Removable media.

- External data storage devices.

- Communication devices.

- Network components, routers, and switches.

- Voice over Internet Protocol (VoIP) equipment.

- GPS equipment.

- Information regarding Internet activity.

- Information regarding steganography.

- Printed e-mail, notes, and letters.

Glossary

Analog: Also spelled analogue. A device or system that represents changing values as continuously variable physical quantities. A typical analog device is a clock on which the hands move continuously around the face. Such a clock is capable of indicating every possible time of day. In contrast, a digital clock is capable of representing only a finite number of times (every 10th of a second, for example).

Bandwidth: The amount of information or data that can be sent over a network connection in a given period of time. Bandwidth is usually stated in bits per second (bps), kilobits per second (kbps), or megabits per second (mps).

Bit-by-bit duplicate copy: The process of copying data stored on digital media so that it replicates the data at the lowest level. The term "bit copy" refers to the duplication of the zeros and ones (bits) that are the binary form of digital data.

BIOS: Basic Input Output System. The set of routines stored in read-only memory on a system circuit board that starts a computer, then transfers control to the operating system. The BIOS opens communication channels with computer components such as the hard disk drives, keyboard, monitor, printer, and communication ports.

Blackberry: A handheld device that functions as a cellular phone, personal organizer, wireless Internet browser, speakerphone, long-range digital walkie-talkie, and mini-laptop. Can be used to send and receive e-mail and text messages.

Blog: Derived from Weblog. A series of online journal entries posted to a single Web page in reverse-chronological order. Blogs generally represent the personality of the author or reflect the purpose of the Web site that hosts the blog.

BMP: A filename extension for Bitmap, an image file format generally used to store digital images or pictures.

Buffer: A block of memory that holds data temporarily and allows data to be read or written in larger chunks to improve a computer's performance. The buffer is used for temporary storage of data read from or waiting to be sent to a device such as a hard disk, CD-ROM, printer, or tape drive.

Cables: A collection of wires or optical fibers bound together, used as a conduit for components and devices to communicate or transfer data.

CAT-5/Category-5: A cable capable of transmitting data at high speeds (100 megabits per second and faster). CAT-5 cables are commonly used for voice and data applications in the home.

CAT-5e: Enhanced CAT-5. Similar to a CAT-5 cable, but with improved specifications.

CAT-6/Category-6 (ANSI/TIA/EIA-568-B.2-1): A cable standard for Gigabit Ethernet and other interconnect that is backward compatible with CAT-5, CAT-5e and Cat-3 cables. A Cat-6 cable features more stringent specifications for crosstalk and system noise. The cable standard is suitable for 10BASE–T, 100BASE–TX, and 1000BASE–T (Gigabit Ethernet) connections.

CD/CD-ROM: Compact Disc—Read-Only Memory. A compact disc that contains data accessible by a computer.

CD-R: Compact Disc—Recordable. A disc to which data can be written but not changed or erased.

CD-RW: Compact Disc—Rewritable. A disc to which data can be written, rewritten, changed, and erased.

Chat Room: An Internet client that allows users to communicate in real time using typed text, symbols, or audio.

Compact Flash Card: A small, removable mass storage device that relies on flash memory technology—a storage technology that does not require a battery to retain data indefinitely. There are two types of compact flash cards: Type I cards are 3.3mm thick; Type II cards are 5.5mm thick.

Compressed File: A file that has been reduced in size by use of an algorithm that removes or combines redundant data for ease of transfer. A compressed file is generally unreadable to most programs until the file is uncompressed.

Cookies: Small text files on a computer that store information about what information a user accessed while browsing the Internet.

CPU: Central Processing Unit. The computer microprocessing chip that contains several thousand to several million transistors that perform multiple functions simultaneously.

Deleted Files: Files no longer associated with a file allocation table or master file table. Deleted files are still resident on the media but are not accessible by the operating system.

DHCP: Dynamic Host Configuration Protocol. A set of rules used by communications devices such as computers, routers, or network adapters to allow the device to request and obtain an IP address from a server that has a list of addresses available for assignment.

Digital (photographs, video, audio): A digital system uses discrete values rather than the continuous spectrum values of analog. The word "digital" can refer to the type of data storage and transfer, the internal working of a device, or the type of display.

Digital Camera: A still camera that records images in digital format. Unlike traditional analog cameras that record infinitely variable intensities of light, digital cameras record discrete numbers for storage on a flash memory card or optical disk.

Digital Evidence: Information stored or transmitted in binary form that may be introduced and relied on in court.

DivX: A brand name of products created by DivX, Inc., including the DivX Codec, which has become popular due to its ability to compress lengthy video segments into small sizes while maintaining relatively high visual quality. It is one of several codecs, or digital data encoding and decoding programs, commonly associated with ripping, where audio and video multimedia are transferred to a hard disk and transcoded. As a result, DivX has been a center of controversy because of its use in the replication and distribution of copyrighted DVDs.

Docking Station: A device that enables laptop and notebook computers to use peripheral devices and components normally associated with a desktop computer such as scanners, keyboards, monitors, and printers.

Documentation: Written notes, audio or videotapes, printed forms, sketches, or photographs that form a detailed record of a scene, the evidence recovered, and actions taken during the search of a scene.

Dongle: A copy protection or security device supplied with software. The dongle hinders unauthorized use or duplication of software because each copy of the program requires a dongle to function.

DSL: Digital Subscriber Line. A high-speed digital modem technology that allows high-speed data communication over existing telephone lines between end users and telephone companies.

DVD: Digital Versatile Disk. A high-capacity compact disk that can store up to 28 times the amount of data that a standard CD-ROM can hold. DVDs are available in DVD-R, DVD-RW, DVD+R, DVD+RW, and BlueRay formats.

Electromagnetic Field: The field of force associated with electric charge in motion that has both electric and magnetic components and contains a definite amount of electromagnetic energy. Speakers and radio transmitters frequently found in the trunks of patrol cars are examples of devices that produce electromagnetic fields.

Electronic Device: A device that operates on principles governing the behavior of electrons. Examples of electronic devices include computer systems, scanners, and printers.

Electronic Evidence: Information or data of investigative value that is stored on or transmitted by an electronic device.

Electronic Storage Device: Any medium that can be used to record information electronically. Examples include hard disks, magnetic tapes, compact discs, videotapes, and audiotapes. Examples of removable storage devices include thumb drives, smart media, flash cards, floppy disks, and Zip® disks.

Encryption: Any procedure used in cryptography to convert plain text into cipher text to prevent anyone but the intended recipient with the corresponding key from reading that data.

EPROM: Erasable programmable read-only memory. A type of computer memory chip that retains its data when its power supply is switched off. Once programmed, an EPROM can be erased only by exposing it to strong ultraviolet light.

Ethernet: The standard local area network (LAN) access method that connects electronic devices to a network, cable modem, or DSL modem for Internet access.

Exculpatory Evidence: Evidence that shows that a criminal charge is not substantiated by the evidence.

Faraday: A dimensionless unit of electric charge quantity, equal to approximately 6.02×10^{23} electric charge carriers. This is equivalent to one mole, also known as Avogadro's constant. Faraday isolation bags are used to prevent mobile phones and devices from connecting to communication signals.

File Format: Refers to file type based on file structure, layout, or how a particular file handles the information (sounds, words, images) contained within it. A file's format is usually indicated by the three- or four-letter file extension in the MS-DOS filename, e.g., .doc or .jpg.

Firewall: A firewall allows or blocks traffic into and out of a private network or a user's computer, and is the primary method for keeping a computer secure from intruders. Also used to separate a company's public Web server from its internal network and to keep internal network segments secure.

FireWire: A high-speed serial bus that allows for the connection of up to 63 devices. Widely used for downloading video from digital camcorders to the computer.

First Responder: The initial responding law enforcement officer or other public safety official to arrive at a scene.

GPS: Global Positioning System. A system of satellites and receiving devices used to compute positions on Earth. GPS is used in navigation and real estate assessment surveying.

GIF: Graphics Interchange Format. One of the two most common file formats for graphic images; the other is the jpg. Widely used on the Internet due to its high compression and subsequent small file size. GIF files have a .gif file extension and can be created or edited in most popular graphics applications.

Hard Copy: A permanent reproduction of data on any media suitable for direct use by a person, e.g., printed pages and facsimile pages.

Hard Drive: A data storage device that consists of an external circuit board; external data and power connections; and internal glass, ceramic, or magnetically charged metal platters that store data. The most common types of hard drives are IDE and SCSI.

Hardware: The physical components that make up a computer system such as the keyboard, monitor, and mouse.

Header: In many disciplines of computer science, a header is a unit of information that precedes a data object. In a network transmission, a header is part of the data packet and contains transparent information about the file or the transmission. In file management, a header is a region at the beginning of each file where bookkeeping information is kept. The file header may contain the date the file was created, the date it was last updated, and the file's size. The header can be accessed only by the operating system or by specialized programs.

Hidden Data: Many computer systems include an option to protect information from the casual user by hiding it. A cursory examination of the system may not display hidden files, directories, or partitions to the untrained viewer. A forensic examination will document the presence of this type of information.

Host: A computer on a network that provides resources or services to other computers on the same network. One host machine may provide several services, such as SMTP (e-mail) and HTTP (Web).

IM: Instant Messenger. A type of communications service that enables users to communicate in real time over the Internet. Analogous to a telephone conversation but communication is text-based.

Internet Protocol (IP) Address: A 32-bit binary number that uniquely identifies a host connected to the Internet or to other Internet hosts for communication through the transfer of data packets. An IP address is expressed in "dotted quad" format consisting of decimal values of its four bytes separated with periods, e.g.,127.0.0.1.

IRC: Internet Relay Chat. A multiuser Internet chat client through which users communicate on channels referred to as chat rooms.

ISDN: Integrated Services Digital Network. A high-speed digital telephone line Internet connection.

ISP: Internet Service Provider. A business that provides access to the Internet. Small Internet service providers provide service via modem and ISDN, while larger ones also offer private line hookups.

JPG: Joint Photographic Experts Group. Also JPEG. A compression technique used for saving images and photographs. Reduces the file size of the images without reducing their quality; widely used on the World Wide Web.

Latent: Present, although not visible, but capable of becoming visible.

MAC Address: Also known as the hardware address or ethernet address. A unique identifier specific to the network card inside a computer. Allows the DHCP server to confirm that the computer is allowed to access the network. MAC addresses are written as XX–XX–XX–XX–XX–XX, where the Xs represent digits or letters from A to F.

Magnetic Media: Includes hard disk drives, tapes, cartridges, diskettes, or cassettes used to store data magnetically.

Media Storage Devices: Examples include disk drives, tape drives, Zip® drives, thumb drives, floppy disks, CDs, and DVDs. Unlike main memory, media storage devices retain data even when the computer is turned off.

Memory Card: A removable data storage device commonly used for storing images in digital cameras but can also be used to store any type of data. These devices are made up of nonvolatile flash memory chips in various forms such as CompactFlash, SmartMedia, and Memory Stick.

MiniDV: A videocassette designed for use in MiniDV digital camcorders. MiniDV cassettes can have up to 530 lines of video resolution.

MP3: An acronym for MPEG-1 or MPEG-2 audio layer 3. MP3 is the file extension for MPEG audio layer 3. Layer 3 is one of three coding schemes for the compression of audio signals. Layer 3 uses perceptual audio coding and psychoacoustic compression to remove the redundant and irrelevant parts of a sound signal.

MPEG: Moving Picture Experts Group. A standard for compressing full motion video. MPEG files frequently have an .mpg file extension.

Multimedia Player: A hard disk or flash memory-based electronic device, such as an MP3 player, capable of storing and playing files in one or more media formats including: MPEG, DivX, and Xvid, audio, MP3, WAV, Ogg Vorbis, BMP, JPEG, GIF, images, and interactive media Adobe Flash and Flash LITE.

Network: A configuration of independent computers, peripherals, and devices connected through data communication wires or wireless technologies capable of sharing information and resources.

Network Connection: A wired or wireless communication link between a group of computers or devices for the purpose of sharing information and resources.

Ogg Vorbis: An open-source audio encoding and streaming technology.

Operating System: A computer program that controls the components of a computer system and facilitates the operation of applications. Microsoft® Windows® Me, Microsoft® Windows® XP, Vista®, Linux, and Apple® MacOS are common operating systems.

Original Electronic Evidence: Physical devices and the data contained by those items at the time of seizure.

Palm: Any of the various models of personal digital assistants marketed by Palm, Inc.

Password-Protected File: A file configured to deny access to users who do not enter the correct password (a specific character or combination of characters). Access denial security does not modify the content of the file; it only prevents those without the password from accessing it.

PCMCIA: Personal Computer Memory Card International Association. A trade association responsible for promulgating standards for integrated circuit cards, including PC cards and Express Cards.

PCMIA: Personal Computer Manufacturer Interface Adaptor. Used to expand the function of personal computers.

PDA: Personal Digital Assistant. A handheld device that can function as a cellular phone, fax sender, and personal organizer. Many PDAs incorporate handwriting and voice recognition features. Also referred to as a palmtop, handheld computer, or pocket computer.

Peripheral: Any device used in a computer system that is not part of the essential computer, i.e., the memory and microprocessor. Peripheral devices can be external such as a mouse, keyboard, printer, monitor, external Zip® drive or scanner; or internal such as a CD-ROM drive, CD-R drive, or internal modem.

Personal Computer (PC): A computer whose price, size, and capabilities make it useful for individuals.

Phishing: Internet fraud perpetrated through an e-mail linking to a Web site simulating a legitimate financial organization; once on the fake Web site, victims are tricked into revealing a security access code, credit card or Social Security number, user ID, or password, which is then used by the thieves to steal the victim's financial resources.

Phreaking: Telephone system hacking.

Printer Cable: A cable that connects a printer to a computer.

Port: An interface by which a computer communicates with another device or system. Personal computers have various types of ports. Internally, there are several ports for connecting disk drives, display screens, and keyboards. Externally, personal computers have ports for connecting modems, printers, mice, and other peripheral devices.

Port Replicator: A device that contains common computer ports (e.g., serial, parallel, and network ports) that plug into a notebook computer. A port replicator is similar to a docking station but docking stations normally provide capability for additional expansion boards.

Printer Spool File: The temporary file created when a print command is executed.

Processor: The logic circuitry that responds to and processes the basic instructions that drive a computer. The term processor has generally replaced the term central processing unit (CPU). The processor in a personal computer or that is embedded in small devices is often called a microprocessor.

PS2: PlayStation 2. A popular video game console.

PSP: PlayStation Portable. A handheld videogame console released in 2005 by Sony. Uses a Universal Media Disc and Memory Stick PRO Duo card for storage. The PSP also plays music and displays photos.

Quarantine: The status of any item or material isolated while pending a decision on its use.

RAM: Random Access Memory. Computer memory that stores data and can be accessed by the processor without accessing the preceding bytes, enabling random access to the data in memory.

Remote: Files, devices, and other resources that are not connected directly to a computer.

Removable Media: Items that store data and can be easily removed from a computer system or device such as floppy disks, CDs, DVDs, cartridges, and data backup tape.

Screen Name: The name a user chooses to use when communicating with others online. A screen name can be a person's real name, a variation of the person's real name, or it can be a pseudonym (handle). Screen names are required for instant messaging (IM) applications.

Screen Saver: A utility program that prevents a monitor from being etched by an unchanging image. It also can provide access control.

Seizure Disk: A specially prepared floppy disk configured to boot a computer system and protect it from accidental or unintentional alteration of data.

Serial Cable: Provided with a digital camera. Used to connect a digital camera to a personal computer so that images can be downloaded on to the computer hard disk.

Server: A computer that provides some service for other computers connected to it via a network.

SIM: Subscriber Identity Module. The SIM card is the smart card inserted into GSM cellular phones. The SIM identifies the user account to the network, handles authentication, and provides data storage for basic user data and network information. It may also contain some applications that run on a compatible phone.

Sleep Mode: Also Suspend Mode. A power conservation state that suspends power to the hard drive and monitor; results in a blank screen.

Smart Card: Also chip card, or integrated circuit card. A pocket-sized card with embedded integrated circuits which can process information. There are two broad categories of smart cards. Memory cards contain only nonvolatile memory storage components, and perhaps some specific security logic. Microprocessor cards contain volatile memory and microprocessor components.

Software: Computer programs designed to perform specific tasks, such as word processing, accounting, network management, Web site development, file management, or inventory management.

Stand-Alone Computer: A computer not connected to a network or other computer.

Steganography: The process of hiding files within other files.

System Administrator: A user who has the most comprehensive access privileges over a computer system.

Temporary and Swap Files: To improve computer performance, many computer operating systems and applications
temporarily store data from system memory or RAM in files
on the hard drive. These files, which are generally hidden and
inaccessible, may contain information useful to the investigator.

Thumbnail: A miniature representation of a page or an image
used to identify a file by its contents. Clicking the thumbnail
opens the file. Thumbnails are an option in file managers, such
as Windows Explorer, and they are found in photo editing and
graphics program to quickly browse multiple images in a folder.

Touch Screen: A video display screen that has a touch-sensitive
transparent panel covering the screen. A user can touch the
screen to activate computer functions instead of using a point-
ing device such as a mouse or light pen.

USB: Universal Serial Bus. A computer hardware interface
connection that facilitates the use of many peripheral devices
including keyboards, mice, joysticks, scanners, printers, external storage devices, mobile phones, smart phones, PDAs, and
software dongles.

Virus: A software program capable of spreading and repro-
ducing itself on connected computers and damaging or cor-
rupting legitimate computer files or applications.

VoIP: Voice over Internet Protocol. The technology used to
transmit voice conversations over a data network using the
Internet protocol. Data network may be the Internet or a
corporate Intranet.

Volatile Memory: Memory that loses its content when
power is turned off or lost.

WAV: An abbreviation of WAVeform. A type of audio file.
Usually has a .wav file extension.

Wireless: Any computing device that can access a network
without a wired connection.

Wireless Modem: A modem that accesses a wireless telephone system to provide a connection to a network.

Wireless Router: A network device that consists of a wireless access point (base station), a wired LAN switch, and a router to connect computers and peripheral devices to an Internet service. Wireless routers are a convenient way to connect a small number of wired and any number of wireless computers to the Internet.

Write Protection: Software or hardware that prevents data from being written to a storage device. Write protection ensures that digital evidence is not modified after it is seized.

Xvid: An open-source video codec library (video compression software) that follows the MPEG–4 standard.

Zip®: A removable 3.5-inch data storage disk drive.

Zip® File: A file that has been reduced in size to allow faster transfer between computers or to save storage space. Some compressed files have a .exe file extension, which indicates that the file is self-extracting.

The National Institute of Justice is the
research, development, and evaluation
agency of the U.S. Department of Justice.
NIJ's mission is to advance scientific research,
development, and evaluation to enhance the
administration of justice and public safety.

The National Institute of Justice is a component of
the Office of Justice Programs, which also includes
the Bureau of Justice Assistance; the Bureau of
Justice Statistics; the Community Capacity
Development Office; the Office for Victims of
Crime; the Office of Juvenile Justice and
Delinquency Prevention; and the Office of Sex
Offender Sentencing, Monitoring, Apprehending,
Registering, and Tracking (SMART).

www.ingramcontent.com/pod-product-compliance
Lightning Source LLC
Chambersburg PA
CBHW071619170526
45166CB00003B/1119